World Art

Sue Nicholson

QED Publishing

Copyright © QED Publishing 2004

First published in the UK in 2004 by
QED Publishing
A Quarto Group Company
226 City Road
London, EC1V 2TT

www.qed-publishing.co.uk

A Catalogue record for this book
is available from the British Library.

ISBN 1 84538 282 X

Written by Sue Nicholson
Designed by Caroline Grimshaw
Edited by Sian Morgan and Matthew Harvey
Photographer Michael Wicks
Picture Researcher Joanne Beardwell
Artwork Sarah Morley
Calligraphy Che'en-Ling

Creative Director: Louise Morley
Editorial Manager: Jean Coppendale

Printed and bound in China

Picture credits
The Art Archive 6t, 8t, 8c, 10t & b, 14t & b, 24,26;
Corbis/Christie's Images 18t /Robert Holmes 17tc
/Dave G Houser 12 /Reza Webistan 22r, 28r/
Royal Ontario Museum 18b /Dinodia 16, 17tl & c;
Japan National Tourist Organization 20

The words in **bold** are explained in the Glossary on page 30.

Contents

Tools and materials

On this page you can see some of the things you will need to do the projects in this book. Before you begin any of the activities, check to make sure you have everything you need.

1 Sticky tape or masking tape
2 Paper glue
3 Dish of wallpaper paste for papier mâché projects
4 Balloons
5 Paintbrushes
6 Split pins
7 Poster paints
8 Air-drying modelling clay
9 Enamel paint
10 Beads, stick-on gems, sequins, etc.
11 Coloured paper
12 Paint roller
13 Crayons and coloured chalk
14 Pencils
15 Ruler
16 Scissors
17 String
18 Tissue paper
19 Sketch pad
20 Cutting board

Paints and paintbrushes

As well as different coloured poster paint, you will need some white **emulsion** for first coats on clay or papier mâché models. You also need a selection of paintbrushes: a small decorating brush (for glue or to paint large areas), a medium-sized painting brush and a thin brush to paint fine detail.

TAKE CARE!

For some projects in this book you will need help from an adult; when using a craft knife or a hammer and nails, for example. The instructions will tell you when you need to ask for help.

Sketchbook

Keep a sketchbook. Look for ideas in travel guides and history and geography books. Visit museums or galleries and sketch art and craft from different countries and at different times in history.

Dangerous stuff!

Most wallpaper paste contains a **fungicide**, which is poisonous and may cause an allergic reaction in some people. Before you use it, dab a dot of paste on the inside of your wrist and leave it for a few minutes. If your skin becomes irritated, do not use it, or wear thin plastic gloves. Never get wallpaper paste in your eyes, nose or mouth and always wash your hands well after use.

Ancient world art

Many thousands of years ago in the **Stone Age**, people produced some fantastic paintings. Many were made in caves – possibly as decorations for **ceremonies** or religious **shrines**. Follow the simple steps below to recreate a magical Stone-Age animal painting.

WHAT YOU NEED

- Air-drying modelling clay
- Rolling pin
- Sand
- Poster paint
- Black charcoal (optional)
- Cotton wool
- Sandpaper
- **Varnish** (optional)

A Stone-Age cave painting

1 Lightly draw an animal outline, such as a cow, deer, **bison** or elephant on scrap paper. Use a soft pencil and keep the lines simple.

TIP

Draw the animal's legs at an angle, not straight down, so it looks as though it is running.

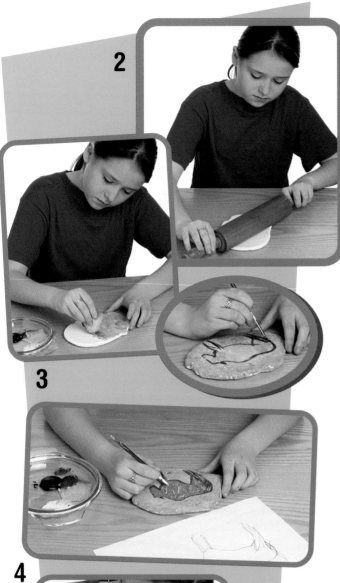

2 Roll out a piece of pale modelling clay (the size of a tennis ball). It doesn't have to be totally smooth. Rub some sand over the clay for a rough surface texture. Then let the clay dry hard.

3 Squirt black and white paint into two separate pools. Mix some to make a light grey, and use cotton wool or a piece of foam to dab it on the clay. When this is dry, paint your animal **outline** in black.

TIP

You can seal your painting with PVA glue mixed with water instead of varnish. Put some PVA glue in a plastic cup. Gradually add water until it is the consistency of single cream. It looks white when you paint it on, but it dries clear.

4 Paint the body in natural colours, such as dark browns and reds.

5 When the paint is dry, gently rub sandpaper over the surface to make it look patchy and old.

6 Add two coats of clear **varnish.** Let the varnish dry between coats.

African mask

Masks are used in all types of African **ceremonies**. Some represent animals or spirits. They are often made of wood and decorated with shells, beads, fabric or animal skins. Here's how to make your own African-style mask.

WHAT YOU NEED
- Pear-shaped balloon
- Newspaper
- Wallpaper paste
- Cardboard
- Sticky tape
- PVA glue
- Poster paints
- Beads, shells, buttons, sequins, raffia and string

African ceremonial masks

1 Blow up a balloon so it is the size of your head, then knot the end.

2 Make a small amount of wallpaper paste, following the instructions on the packet.

8

3 Soak newspaper strips (2–3cm wide and 5–6cm long) in the paste. Lay them across the balloon so that they overlap. Cover just over half the balloon. Add another layer of paper strips and leave it to dry. Repeat until you have eight layers.

4 When the paste is completely dry, pop the balloon with a pin and trim the edges of the paper. Cut out two holes for the eyes.

TIP
Tear the newspaper rather than cutting it. Torn edges lie flatter and overlap more easily.

5 Soak small pieces of paper in water until they break up into bits. Mash the paper with a fork, drain off the water and squeeze until it is almost dry. Mix the pulp with watered-down PVA glue. Use it to build up the eyebrows, nose and mouth.

6 When the glue is dry, paint your mask a brown colour. Pick out the features in dark brown, red and gold paint. Decorate it with shells, beads or buttons. Add hair made of raffia, wool or string.

Egyptian amulet

The **Ancient Egyptians** believed that people's spirits must be reunited with their bodies after they died. They decorated dead bodies with amulets, or lucky charms. In this project, you can make a Wedjat-eye charm, which were used by the Egyptians to ward off evil spirits.

WHAT YOU NEED

- Air-drying modelling clay
- Rolling pin or bottle
- Plastic knife
- Wooden or plastic modelling tools
- Poster paint
- **Varnish** or PVA glue

Ancient Egyptian scarab (beetle) amulets

1 Roll out a piece of clay, until it is 1–2cm thick and about 2cm larger than you want your finished eye to be. Carve the **outline** of an eye on the clay with a modelling tool or pencil. Cut out the shape with a plastic knife.

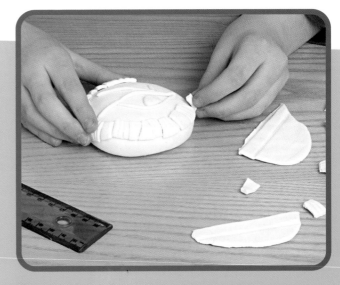

2 Roll out long, thin pieces of clay and press them into the eye shape to build up the design.

3 Use your tools to make patterns in the clay for decoration.

TIP

Everyday household objects, such as a fork, a blunt nail or the end of a paintbrush make great tools.

4 When the model is dry, paint it. Add two coats of varnish (or PVA glue mixed with water). Let the first coat dry before you add the next.

TIP

To get a smooth surface for decorating, paint an undercoat of white **emulsion** paint. Leave this to dry before adding coloured poster paint.

Ancient Greek vase

The best pottery in **Ancient Greece** was made in **Athens**. The clay found near there turned a beautiful reddish-brown when it was fired. The vase in this project is made of papier mâché. It is not watertight.

WHAT YOU NEED
- Large, oval-shaped balloon
- Newspaper
- Wallpaper paste
- Paint and brushes

1 Blow up the balloon. Make some wallpaper paste, then tear sheets of newspaper into strips about 2–3cm wide and 5–6cm long.

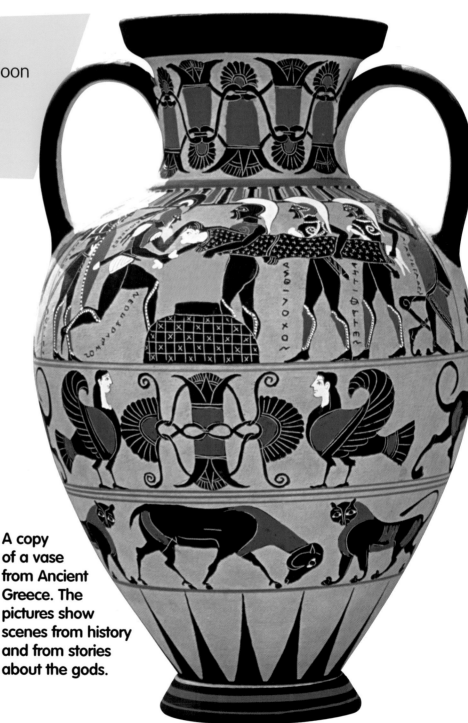

A copy of a vase from Ancient Greece. The pictures show scenes from history and from stories about the gods.

2 Soak the strips in the paste, then lay them over the balloon neatly so that they overlap. Cover the balloon in two layers, then leave it to dry.

3 Repeat until you have eight layers. When the paste is dry, pop the balloon with a pin.

4 Cut out a strip of thin card and tape it in a circle to the base of the balloon shape. Attach a wider piece to the top in the same way. Cut two more strips of card and tape them to the sides of the vase for handles.

5 Cover the card base, top and handles with two layers of newspaper strips. Make sure that the strips overlap the main part of the vase. When they are dry, add another layer.

6 When this is dry, paint the vase red-brown. Paint the base, rim and handles of the vase black.

7 Paint a design on the side of your pot in black. This shows an owl – the symbol of the Greek goddess **Athena**. Paint decorative borders top and bottom then, when dry, add a coat of **varnish**.

Roman-style mosaic

Many **Roman** homes had a mosaic – a picture made of tiny glass, stone or tile squares called 'tesserae' – pressed into the floor. Some mosaics showed pictures of the gods or scenes from history.

WHAT YOU NEED

- Squared paper
- Coloured paper, or white paper and poster paints, or old glossy magazines, or gummed coloured paper
- Black sugar paper
- Scissors
- PVA glue

1 Plan your design on squared paper, so the finished design is around 23 x 15cm. Copy this dog mosaic or choose another animal or your initials. Design a border to frame your design.

Roman mosaics

2 Lay the paper with the design on it face down on the sugar paper. Rub the paper with the pencil, so that the design transfers onto the sugar paper.

3 Decide which colours you want to use in your mosaic.

TIPS

- Sort your pieces into colours – blues, greens, reds, and so on.
- Squares cut from magazines give you different **hues** of each of your colours, which gives your design more depth.

4 Cut the paper into pieces, about 1.5 x 1.5cm. You may need to cut some irregular shapes to fit your design. Glue the squares onto the sugar paper. Leave a gap a few millimetres wide between each square.

5 To make your mosaic shine, paint it with PVA glue mixed with water.

TIP

If you want your mosaic to sparkle, cover some squares in glitter glue or paint them in gold or silver metallic paint.

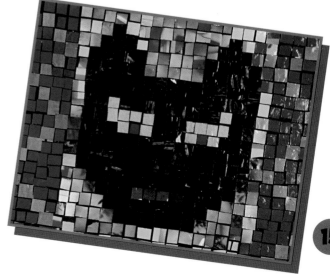

Indian Rangoli

Rangoli is the Indian art of decorating the floor or wall with a **geometric** design, flowers or animals. Intricate Rangoli are painted during **Hindu** festivals, such as **Diwali**, or for birthdays. Each state of India has its own style of Rangoli.

WHAT YOU NEED
- Sketching paper
- Pencil
- White chalk
- Coloured chalk or flour with food colouring

1 Practise drawing small Rangoli on sketching paper. Draw a larger version on a big sheet of paper. Start with a series of evenly spaced dots.

An Indian woman making a Rangoli

2 Join some of the dots to form a geometric pattern, a flower or animal shape. Here are some ideas.

3 Copy your design onto the pavement or playground in chalk or in a flour and water paste (always ask permission first), or draw your Rangoli on a large sheet of black sugar paper.

TIP

Make sure your dots are evenly spaced so that you end up with a regular pattern.

4 Colour your Rangoli with chalk. If you use flour paste, divide the paste into separate bowls and add a couple of drops of different food colouring to each.

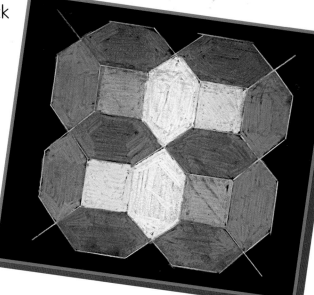

Chinese calligraphy

In China and Japan, calligraphy (beautiful writing produced with a brush) is an art form. Calligraphers spend months practising just one character, or symbol. The Chinese character on the card in this project means 'Peace'.

WHAT YOU NEED

- Paintbrush and paint (optional)
- Pencil
- Red marker pen or paint
- Black marker pen
- Thin white card
- Cream card
- Dark card
- Ruler
- Scissors

1 Draw the outline of the 'Peace' character as shown below on a piece of white card 6 x 6cm, using the grid lines to help you. If you are using a brush, follow the red arrows inside the outlines.

Chinese calligraphy scroll

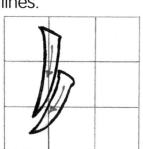

2 If you have drawn pencil outlines, fill them in with a black marker pen. Try to keep within your pencil marks.

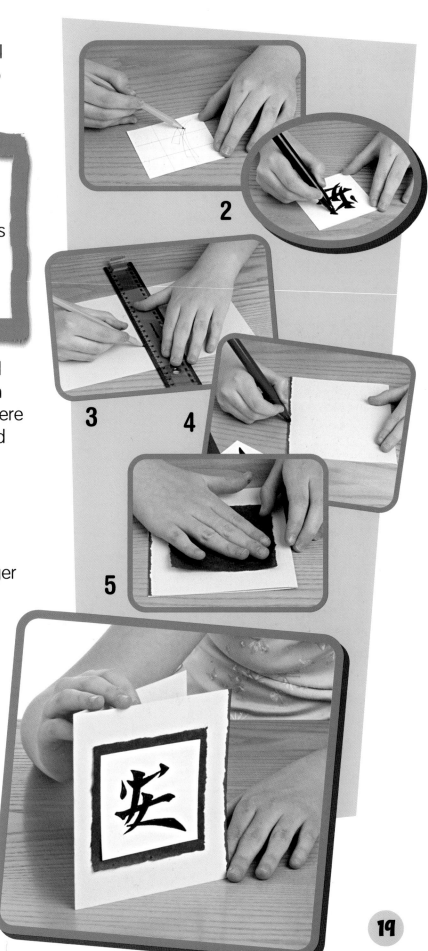

TIP

If you use a brush, try different sizes. A thick, pointed brush makes bold, sweeping strokes. Lift the brush away from the paper to make thin, light brush strokes.

3 Cut out a rectangle of thick, textured cream card, 10 x 14cm. Fold the card in half. To make a neat fold, measure where you want the fold to be with a ruler and mark the line in pencil.

4 Colour the right edge of the card in bright red poster paint or marker pen.

5 Cut a piece of dark card slightly larger than your calligraphy and stick it to the card. Now glue the calligraphy on top, so you can see a border of dark card.

Here are two other Chinese characters to practise. They mean 'Beautiful' (left) and 'Lucky' (right).

Japanese banner

In Japan, on Children's Day, children hang up fish-shaped flags on poles outside their homes to bring them good luck. Here's how to make your own fish banner that you can hang up in your room or classroom.

WHAT YOU NEED
- Coloured tissue paper
- Glue
- Scissors
- Thin card

1 Cut three shapes out of tissue paper, copying the shapes in the picture below. Choose a different colour for each. The fish will fold along the centre, so make sure the pieces are big enough.

Japanese fish banners

2 Glue the tail onto one end of the long section, and the head onto the other end.

3 Use your scissors to cut out lots of semicircles of tissue paper for the scales of the fish.

4 Cut out four large circles and two smaller circles to make the eyes. Glue them to the head of the fish.

TIP
When cutting out the scales, fold the paper over so that you can cut lots of scales in one go.

5 When you have enough scales, add them to the long section of the fish. Glue them from the tail upwards, and slightly overlap each row onto the previous one – just like real fish scales.

6 Fold the fish along the centre and glue the bottom edge together. Glue a ring of card inside the mouth. Your fish is now complete, so find a place to display it.

Indonesian puppets

One of the world's oldest traditions of storytelling, shadow puppets have been popular entertainment in Indonesia for more than 1000 years. They are called Wayang Kulit. Here's how to make your own Indonesian-style shadow puppet.

WHAT YOU NEED

- Paper
- Thick card
- Pencil
- Scissors and craft knife
- Split pins
- Wooden dowel, garden cane or wooden barbecue skewers
- Sticky tape
- White sheet
- Lamp

1 Sketch your puppet design roughly on paper. Give it a long nose, long, curling hair and curving body and legs.

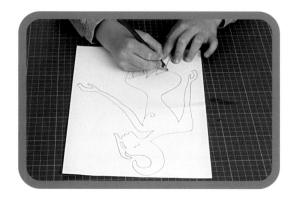

An Indonesian shadow puppet show

2 When you are happy with your design, draw the figure on thick card. Draw the arms separately and divide each arm into two parts – shoulder to elbow, and elbow to hand. Round the ends and cut out all the pieces. Ask an adult for help with the craft knife.

6 To put on a show, suspend a thin white cotton sheet between two chairs. Make sure there are no wrinkles in the sheet. Shine an electric lamp onto the back of the sheet. Kneel down and work the puppet above your head so that your audience see the puppet's shadow. Use one hand to operate one arm, and the other hand to operate the other arm and the head.

3 Tape a stick down the back of one of the puppet's legs, so that the audience cannot see the stick.

5 Tape a thin stick to each of the puppet's hands so that you can move its arms.

4 Join the arms to the body at the shoulder with split pins. Join the lower and upper parts of the arms at the elbow.

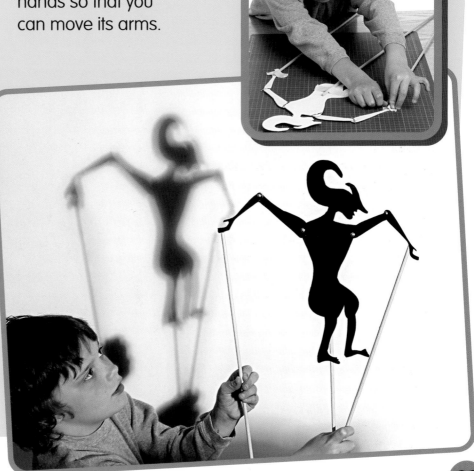

Stained glass

Stained-glass windows decorated churches and cathedrals in **medieval** Europe. Make your own window, and watch it glow when light streams through it.

WHAT YOU NEED

- Black sugar paper
- White pencil
- Craft knife
- Scissors
- Coloured tissue paper or coloured Cellophane
- Glue
- Fine black felt-tip pen

1 Plan your picture first. Keep it simple, with bold lines and leave a 3–4cm border around it for the frame. Now, lightly draw your design on black sugar paper with a white pencil. Leave a gap of 1–2cm between the different colours.

A medieval stained-glass window

TAKE CARE!
You will need an adult to help you with this project.

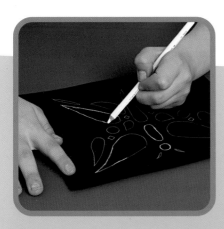

2 Once you are happy with your design, go over the lines again, this time marking them with bold, white **outlines**.

3 Ask an adult to help you cut out your design with a craft knife. Use a cutting board or several layers of newspaper.

4 Cut tissue paper or Cellophane to fit over each window in the paper. Put the pieces in place without glue first to check that they will fit over the holes.

6 Hold the window up to the light. The light will shine through the Cellophane, making the colours glow.

5 Glue each piece onto the back of the paper. Put glue around each hole, and try to keep glue off the front of the window.

TIP

As you cut out more sugar paper, the frame becomes fragile. Keep a heavy book over the frame so that it does not rip while you cut out the remaining pieces.

Arabian tile

Using patterned tiles is one of the main features of art in **Islamic** countries such as Saudi Arabia. In this project, you can make a stencil, then use it to decorate a plain, white tile.

WHAT YOU NEED

- Thick card, 14cm square
- Craft knife
- Masking tape
- Sponge or roller
- Ceramic paint (oil-based or water-based)
- White spirit (for oil-based ceramic paints)
- Plain white tile, 15cm square
- Felt

1 Plan out a tile design and practise drawing it. When you are happy with it, draw it onto a piece of card, 14cm square.

Islamic tiles with geometric shapes and calligraphy

TAKE CARE!

You will need an adult to help you with this project.

2 Ask an adult to help you cut around the lines with a craft knife. Use a cutting board.

3 Tape the edges of the stencil you have made to a plain white ceramic tile.

4 Dab ceramic paint onto the tile through the stencil with a small sponge, brush or roller. Try to fill all the gaps with paint.

TIP

If you use oil-based paint, clean your brushes in white spirit. A cotton bud dipped in white spirit will wipe away mistakes.

5 Remove the stencil. Let the paint dry if it is oil-based, or ask an adult to help you to fire it in the oven if it is water-based (following the instructions on the packet).

6 Cut out a square of felt. Glue it to the back of your tile so you can put it on a table without scratching it.

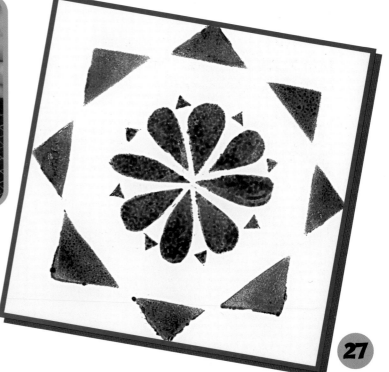

Russian egg

The first Fabergé egg was made in 1885, when the Russian **Tsar**, Alexander III, commissioned a jewelled Easter egg for his wife from the **goldsmith** Carl Fabergé. Here's how to 'blow' a real egg and decorate it in the style of a fabulous Fabergé egg.

WHAT YOU NEED
- Raw hen's or duck's egg
- Pin
- Bowl
- Enamel paints
- Dried lentils, peas or beans
- Stick-on gems

1 Use a pin to push small holes through the top and bottom of the egg.

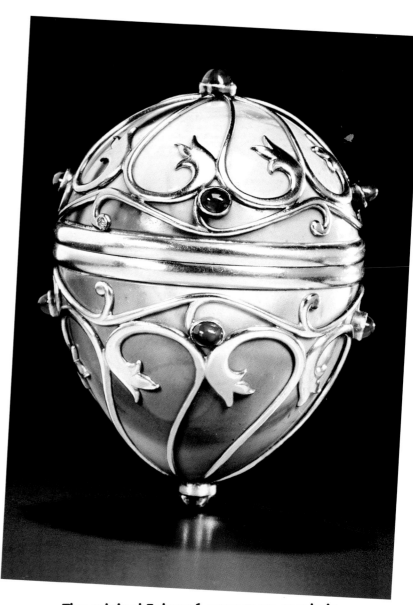

The original Fabergé eggs were made in enamel and decorated with metals, such as silver, gold and copper, and precious stones.

2 Hold the egg over a bowl and gently blow through one of the holes. The contents of the egg will dribble out until the egg is empty.

3 Holding the egg gently, paint the shell.

TIP
Use tweezers to pick up tiny seeds or gems, dip them in PVA glue (or paint a layer of PVA glue on the egg first with a brush), then drop them into place.

4 Decorate the egg using lentils, seeds or stick-on gems for jewels. You can spray-paint the lentils first with gold or silver metallic paint. (If you do this, wear a mask and apron and protect the surfaces you work on.)

5 To make a stand for your egg, wrap an egg cup in coloured tissue paper and decorate it with gems.

Glossary

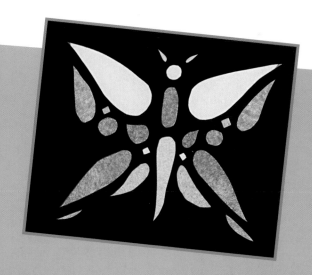

Ancient Egyptians the people who lived in Egypt long ago and built the pyramids

Ancient Greece a civilization of more than 2500 years ago made up of hundreds of cities

Athena the Ancient Greek goddess of wisdom, represented by an owl

Athens the capital of Ancient Greece

bison large, cow-like animal

ceremonies special formal events

Diwali an important Hindu or Sikh festival, held during October or November

emulsion water-based paint for walls

enamel hard, glassy substance for decoration

fungicide poison for killing mould

geometric a pattern made up of regular shapes

goldsmith person who makes gold objects

Hindu relating to one of India's main religions, Hinduism

hues shades or tints of a particular colour

Islamic relating to Islam, one of the world's main religions

medieval relating to the period of history known as the Middle Ages in Europe

outline the outer edge of an object

preserved kept safe from decay

Romans people of Ancient Rome, whose capital was Rome, around 2000 years ago

scarab a type of beetle, sacred to the Ancient Egyptians

shrines sacred places

Stone Age early period of history when humans used stone tools

Tsar the Russian word for emperor

varnish clear paint that dries hard and protects the surface beneath it

Index

Notes for teachers

The world-art projects in this book are aimed at children at Key Stage 2. They can be used as stand-alone lessons or as part of other areas of study. Some of the projects will be useful links with other subjects, such as history or science. While the ideas in the book are offered as inspiration, children should always be encouraged to draw from their imagination and first-hand observation.

SOURCING IDEAS

Encourage children to source their own ideas and references, from books, magazines, travel guides, the Internet, galleries or museums. This will increase their awareness of the roles and purposes of art, craft and design in different times and cultures.

• Use digital cameras to create reference material (museum exhibits, holiday photos, buildings and so on) and use this alongside children's finished work (see below).

• Other lessons can often be an ideal springboard for an art project – for example, a history trip to a museum, a workshop on African music or a story from another country all provide a wealth of ideas. Similarly, encourage children to talk about the types of art they have seen on their holidays, in museums,

at home or during festivals – for example, at Chinese New Year or Diwali.

• Encourage children to keep a sketchbook of their ideas and to collect other images and objects to inspire them.

EVALUATING WORK

Children should share their work with others and compare ideas and methods. Encourage them to talk about their work. How would they change it or do it differently next time? What do they like best/least about it?

• Show the children examples of artists' work at different periods and in different cultures. How did they tackle similar subjects and problems? Do the children like the work? Why? Why not?

• Help children to judge the originality of their work, to appreciate the different qualities in others' work and to value ways of working that are different from their own. Display all the children's work.

GOING FURTHER

Look at ways to develop the projects – children could apply some of the techniques they have learned to make things from other countries. For example, adapt the papier mâché African mask technique to make a South American carnival mask or a Venetian firebird mask. Similarly, children could look at the shape and style of shadow puppets in China and compare them with traditional Indonesian designs.

• Discuss how stories have been created through art in different cultures and at different times – in cave paintings, paintings on Egyptian tombs, Greek vases, Chinese landscape paintings or stained-glass windows. How would children represent their own stories – through sculpture, painting, masks or puppetry?

• Create a large world map for the classroom wall. Attach digital photographs of finished artwork to the countries from which the art originated. Find photographs in books, magazines or travel brochures of other art from those countries and add it to the map as reference material.

• Set up a world-art gallery on your school website.